Witch, Frankenstein, Dracula etc.

HALLOWEEN
COLORING

And many more!

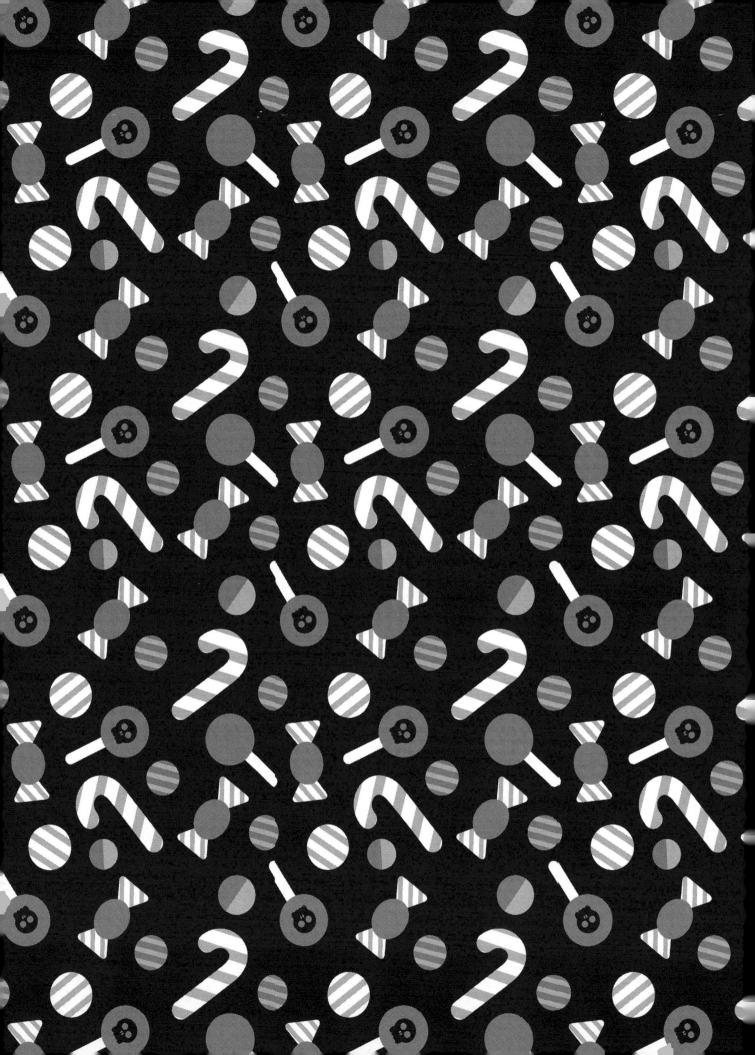

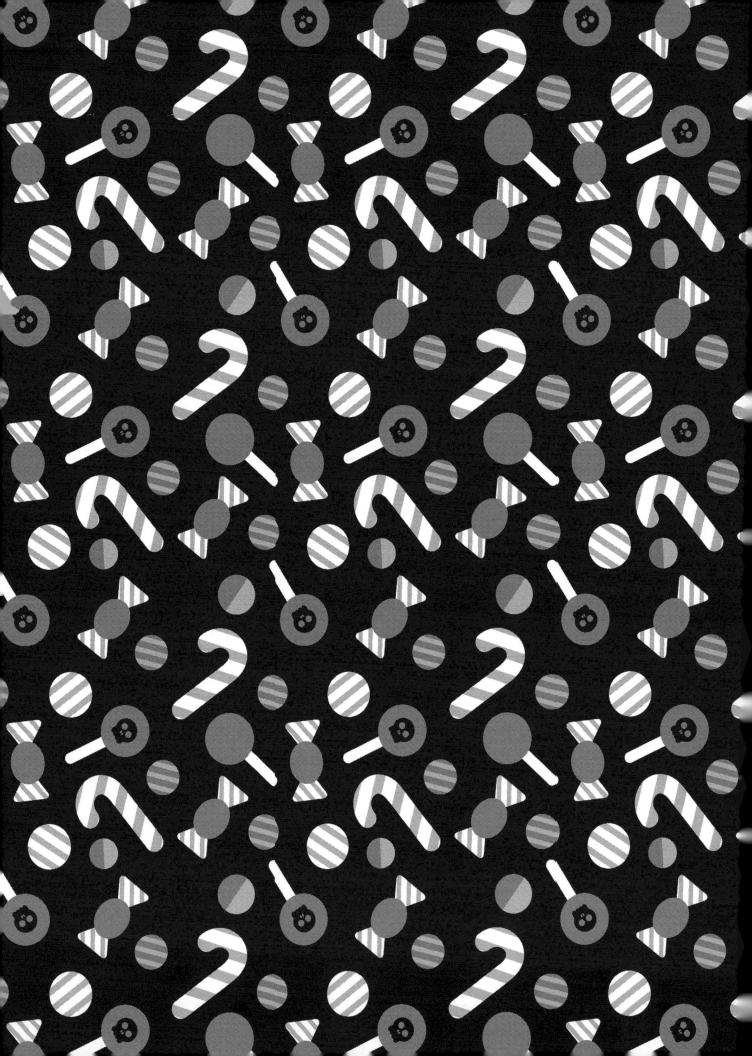

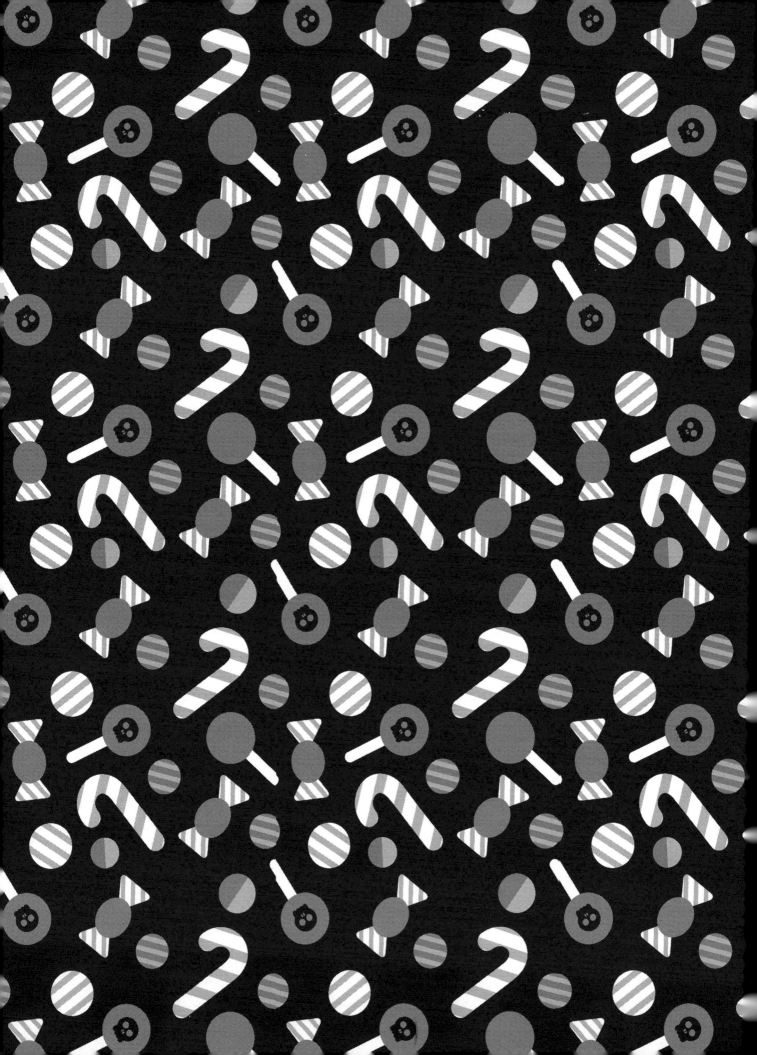

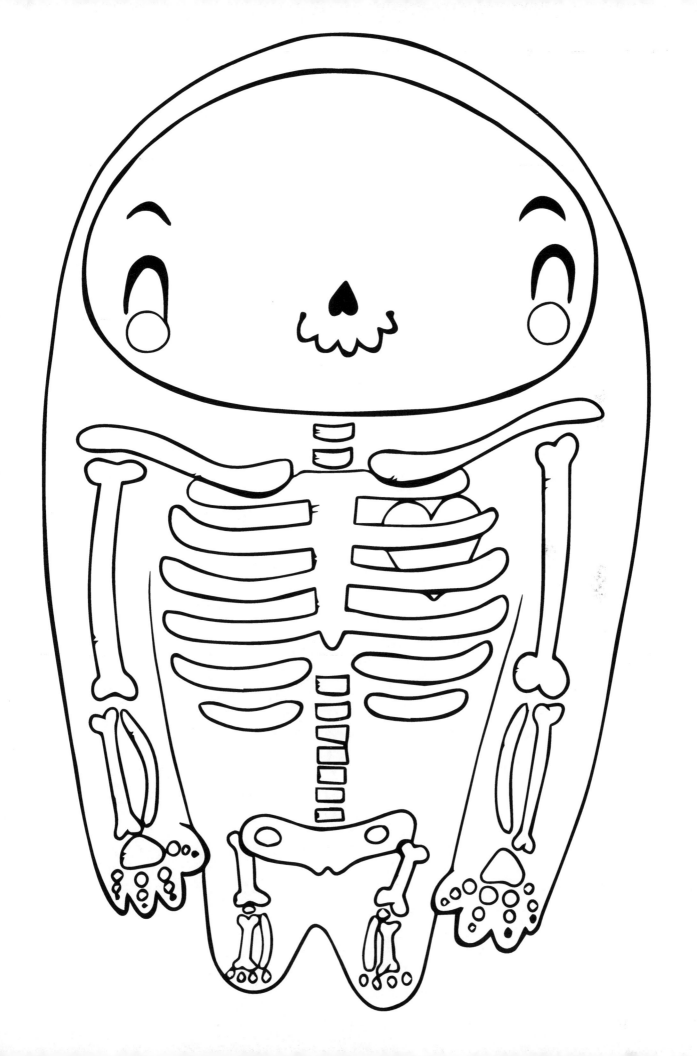

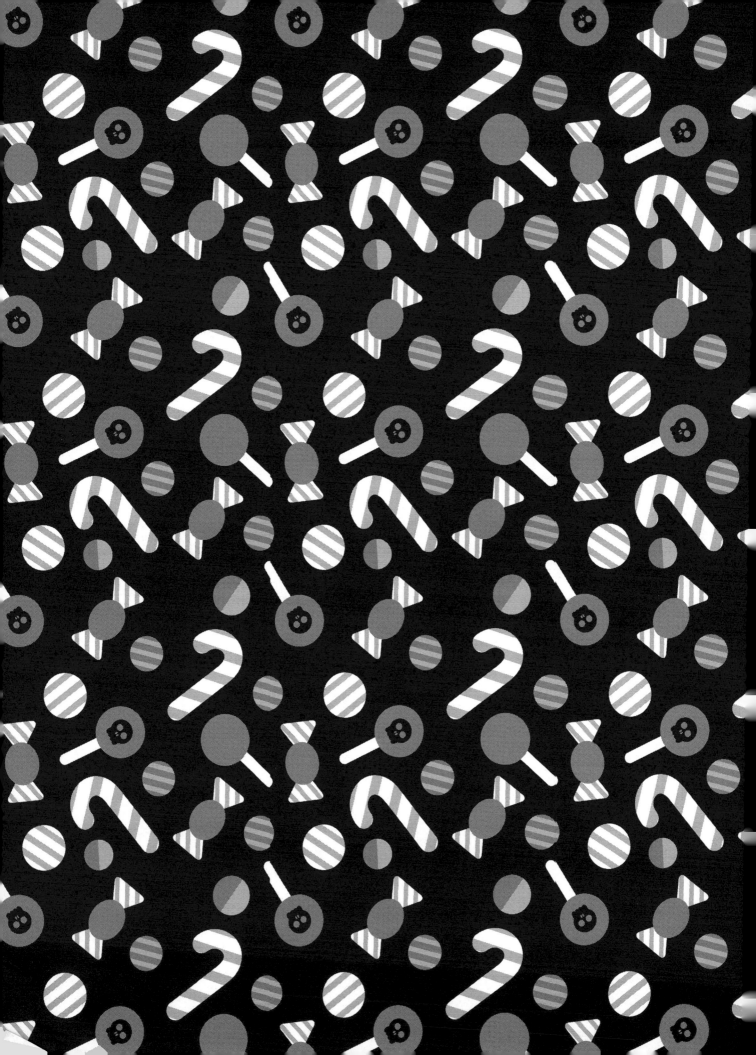

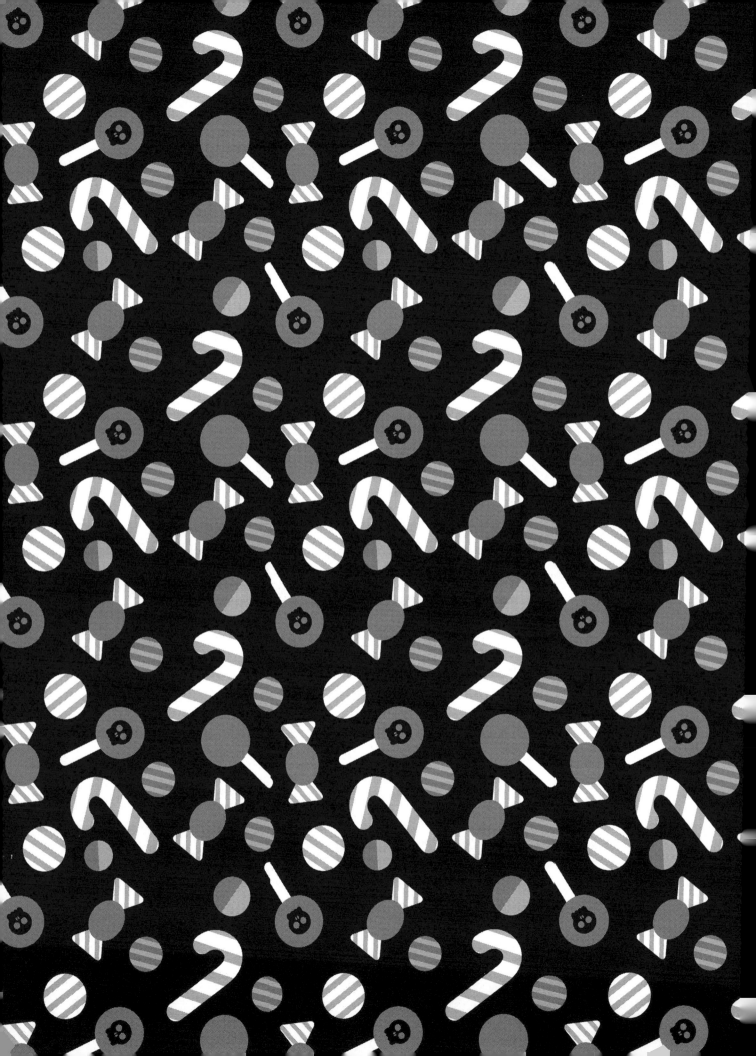

Happy Halloween

Extra page
from our Cute Animal
coloring book for kids

Extra Page
from our Dinosaur
coloring book

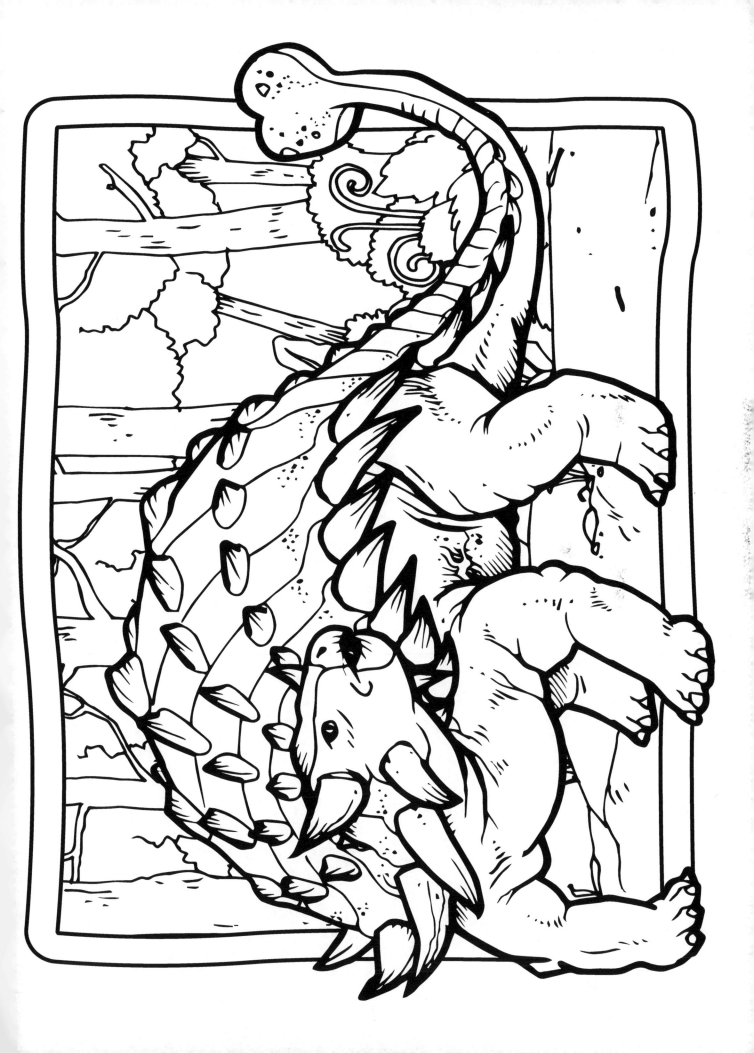

Extra Page
from our
Love & Happiness
coloring book

Extra Page

from our Pirate
coloring book

Leave a review

If you liked our coloring book, please ask your parents to leave a review on Amazon, so we can deliver our lovely coloring boks for more kids.

Available

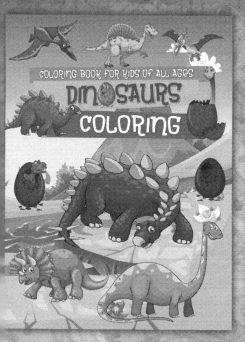

COLORING BOOK FOR KIDS OF ALL AGES
DINOSAURS
COLORING

planetes, astronaut, ufo etc.
infinite space
COLORING

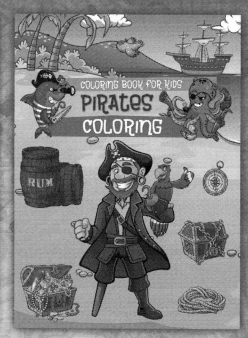

COLORING BOOK FOR KIDS
PIRATES
COLORING

on
Amazon

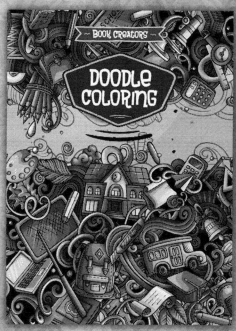

BOOK CREATORS
DOODLE COLORING

COLORING BOOK FOR KIDS OF ALL AGES
LOVE AND JOY
COLORING

COLORING BOOK FOR LITTLE GIRLS
FIARY & MERMAID
COLORING

COLORING BOOK FOR LITTLE GIRLS
CUTE UNICORNS
COLORING

COLORING BOOK FOR KIDS OF ALL AGES
COOL ANIMALS
COLORING

COLORING BOOK FOR KIDS OF ALL AGES
CUTE ANIMALS
COLORING

A-Z WILD ANIMALS COLORING BOOK
WILD ANIMALS
COLORING

COLORING BOOK FOR KIDS OF ALL AGES
SEA WORLD
COLORING

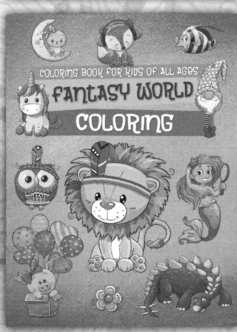

COLORING BOOK FOR KIDS OF ALL AGES
FANTASY WORLD
COLORING

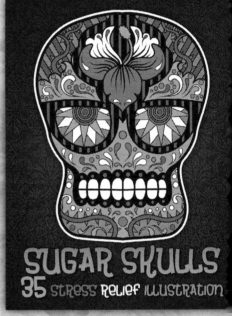

SUGAR SKULLS
35 STRESS RELIEF ILLUSTRATION

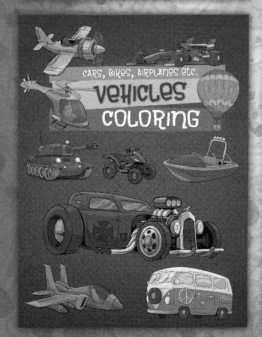

CARS, BIKES, AIRPLANES etc.
VEHICLES
COLORING

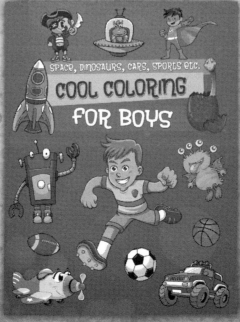

SPACE, DINOSAURS, CARS, SPORTS etc.
COOL COLORING
FOR BOYS

MERMAIDS, FAIRIES, UNICORNS etc.
COLORING BOOK
FOR GIRLS

We hope you have enjoyed our Halloween Coloring Book as much as we enjoyed working on it. If so, please leave a review in our book's page on the Amazon website.

This helps us to create new and better books for you.

Thank you for your support and coloring with us!

www.bookcreators.net
www.twitter.com/bookcreators
www.facebook.com/bookcreators
www.instagram.com/welovemakingbooks

51740016R00044

Made in the USA
San Bernardino, CA
02 September 2019